Doktor Bey's
Bedside
Bug Book

Doktor Bey's Bedside Bug Book

with text and collages by

Derek Pell

A Harvest/HBJ Book
Harcourt Brace Jovanovich · New York and London

Requests for permission to make copies of any part of the work
should be mailed to: Permissions, Harcourt Brace Jovanovich, Inc.,
757 Third Avenue, New York, New York 10017.

Printed in the United States of America

Library of Congress Cataloging in Publication Data

Pell, Derek.
    Doktor Bey's bedside bug book.
    (A Harvest/HBJ book)
    1. Insects—Anecdotes, facetiae, satire, etc.
I. Title.
PN6231.I56P4   818'.5'407   78–6574
ISBN 0–15–626115–4

First Harvest/HBJ edition 1978
A B C D E F G H I J

For my mother and father
&
Sam Mitnick

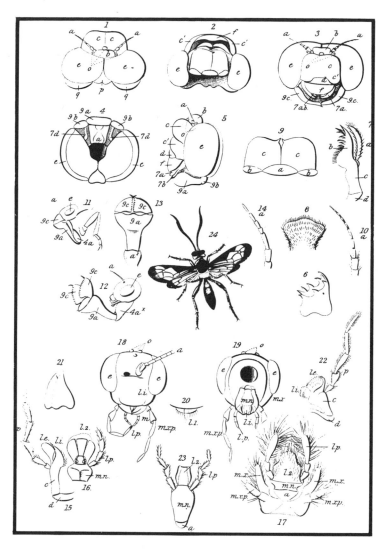

Of all Doktor Bey's many books, the Bedside Bug Book *remains his personal favorite, and understandably so;
for it was his first effort. In 1893, young Bey self-published
this extraordinary volume in a limited edition of five copies,
each signed by the author and bound in silkworm
(Bombyx mori). Unfortunately, there remains no trace
of the original edition, a fact that greatly saddens its
creator. We know that the first edition fell prey
to bookworms, and the good Doktor now regularly uses
fumigators.*

*"Just think of the price a university would've paid,"
remarked Bey during our first meeting at his home in
Cairo. "I'd have been a wealthy man!"*

*Myself included, since I have acted as his exclusive
literary agent for the past forty years, an occupation that,
until recently, was an invitation to Debtor's Prison. I,
too, am filled with remorse. I, too, could have been wealthy.
Of course, my faith in his genius has never flagged, and if
it did, I choose not to recall it. I knew in my heart of hearts
that I had in Doktor Bey a true* original, *yet my creditors
remained skeptical. "He's a deadweight, darling," instructed
my wife on countless occasions, adding demurely: "Drop
him." Yet I persisted. Doktor Bey persisted. My wife ran
off with a legionnaire.*

*Digressions aside, I have been handsomely subsidized
by the publisher to introduce this* unintroducible *volume,
a masterpiece of historical desecration, a drama of dreams,
nightmares, and misplaced dates—a book for the bedside,
a mirror for the basement of our social conscience, an
anthropological bidet! In other words, the* Truth. *Yes,
here is a book unafraid to chronicle the transgressions of
the human race—irrespective of inaccuracy, innuendo, and
(on occasion) vivid distortion—so as to advance the cause of
universal justice.*

Perhaps.

*In hope of discovering a shortcut to the conclusion of
this prelude, I recently returned to Egypt and asked the
author pointblank: "But what, in essence, does the book
mean?" The old man sat in silence for many minutes, then
smiled, winked, and left the room.*

His message was clear.

*Quite frankly, I know what Doktor Bey is getting at, but
it would be most unwise to reveal it now. Each reader must
discover it for himself. As for me, I will simply wish the
reader pleasant dreams and, here, turn out the light.*

*Derek Pell
Weymouth, England
March 2, 1978*

Doktor Bey's Bedside Bug Book

Our saga begins many aeons ago. . . .
An eerie mist illuminated the heavens, heralding
the Birth of Bug! With winged innocence Bug pierced
the skies amid the glowing haze, unaware of its
transcendent destiny.

In the year 13 B.C., Man encountered Bug, and vice versa. To human eyes bulging with ignorance, the insect was seen as an awful apparition that inspired fits of madness and a peculiar form of religious paranoia. A poll taken at the time revealed that 50 percent of the population both feared and worshipped Bug, while the other half had "no comment"—secretly believing it to be an absurd hoax of the gods.

Centuries crept uneventfully by as Man and Bug, for the most part, maintained their distance. However, despite this détente, there was talk among some of going to war against the insect minority—it was growing daily and might move next door and wish to intermarry.

During the period 13 B.C.–1469 A.D., a queer uneasiness grew in the heart of Humanity. Malice squirmed upon the grapevine. Gossip gushed. Bug-jokes spread from village to hamlet. Vile epithets such as **bugger**, **pest**, and **fly-by-night** *were common-place on the tongues of men and women. Children, too, were encouraged to step on ants, while their parents swatted flies in public. Anything that crept, flew, or buzzed was suspect. Superstitions born of pure prejudice became grotesque gospel, and the ludicrous belief that "they all look alike" was rampant.* **Something dark and rotten was afoot.**

Deep in the umbrageous jungles of Africa,
an exception to Man's superstition existed. . . .

A tranquil tribe known as the Uh-pods had made peace
with their bugs. Together, they lived in harmony, wor-
shipping the same one-armed ikon, Vegus.

Here in this heathen Utopia, Bug and Uh-pod bathed together in the sacred river,

enjoyed water sports,

shared intimate moments,

worked side by side on awesome projects,

and rode united into battle.

Unfortunately, less liberal tribes dominated the Continent.

*A strange cult called the Creepwi idolized the bug-head.
The Creepwi tribesmen were expert hunters, and, having
captured an insect, they would deftly separate the head
from its body by a crude process known as* decapitation.
*The carcass, believed to be valueless, was discarded,
while the skull was promptly hung in a nearby tree for
good luck.*

Frequently the Creepwi chief would don a bug-head and preside over a mystical ceremony that lasted six weeks.

Bug-eating tribes became prevalent.

The Gluti, for instance, held little spiritual regard for insect heads or any other individual portion of bug anatomy, but rather consumed them whole— without even the dignified accompaniment of liquid refreshment!

*Elaborate rituals of spicing and dicing
were favored by some.*

*It is rumored that the Gluti had in their possession
an unusual gourmet cookbook.*

*The most notorious cannibals gloried
in the multitude of bugs consumed and
actually kept records of their number
by erecting lines of stones. One such
gourmand totted up eight hundred
seventy-two, and the Christian son of
this ogre declared that his father ate
them all himself, allowing no one to share
with him. Another member of the same
family had registered forty-seven when
his conversion to Christianity put a stop to
the amusement and compelled him to be
satisfied with human flesh.*

Meanwhile,

**back in Civilization, bug life
was no less a nightmare. In England,
insects were falsely accused of hei-
nous crimes and imprisoned alongside
dangerous lunatics.**

Throughout Europe, torture flourished.

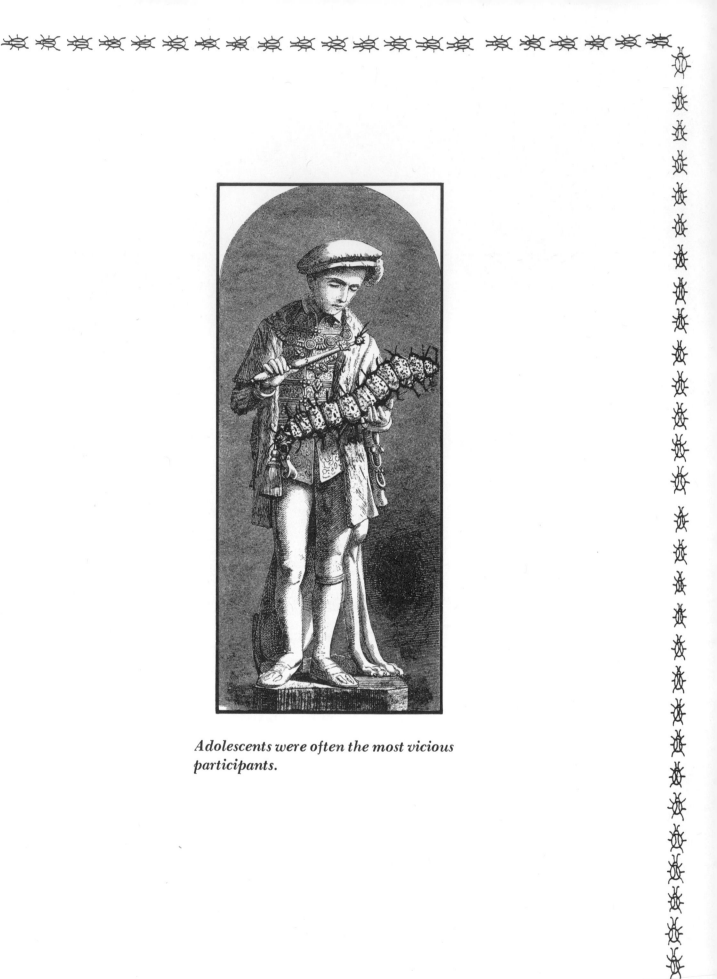

Adolescents were often the most vicious participants.

Insects seemingly lay resigned to their fate.

Eventually men grew bored with the traditional tools of torment . . .

and new implements were invented.

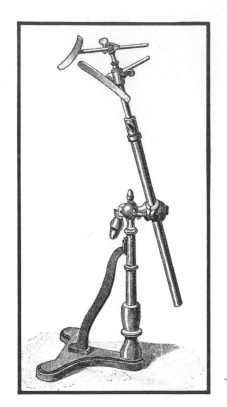

*In some areas of the world, bugs
served as props for sadistic sports.*

There was soon competition among nations to see which could devise the most wicked machine.

France's contribution was the "Outdoor Grill."

The British favored the "Bug-Warmer."

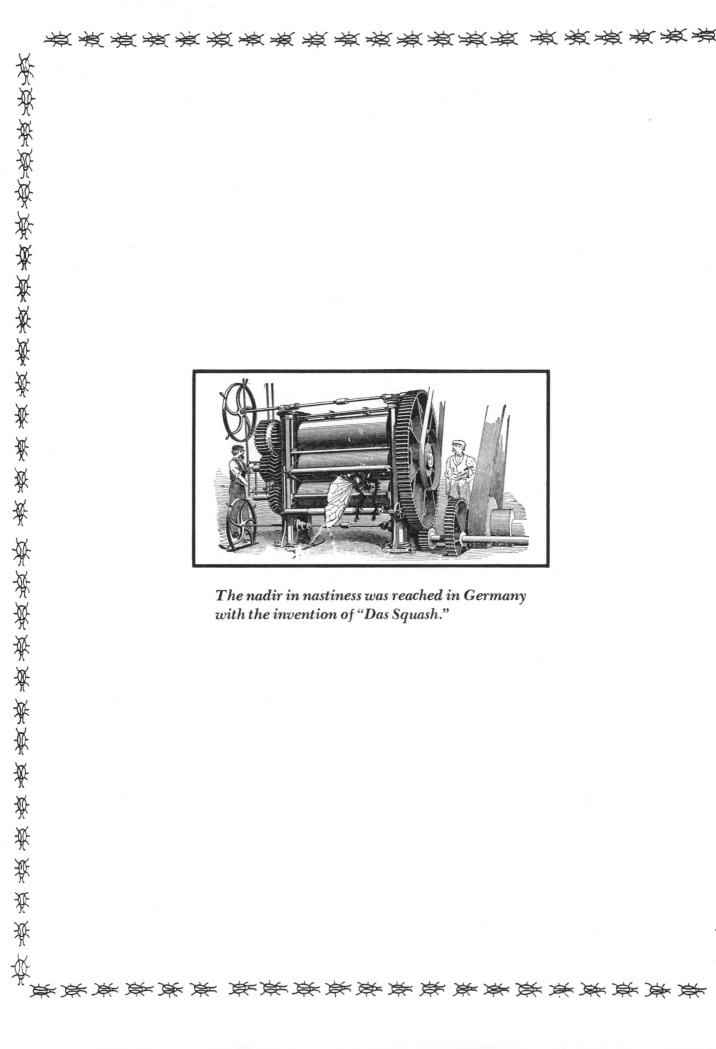

The nadir in nastiness was reached in Germany with the invention of "Das Squash."

In America,

bugs were discovered to be
of commercial value. On April 1, 1778,
in Boston, the insect made its début in
the marketplace.

The bug market became a festive garden for Capitalists.
Unlicensed street vendors displayed colorful
species at a discount. Clearly, they were contraband.

While certain bugs were bartered as curiosities,

others were exploited as valuable collectors' items.

The most beautiful ones were often the cause of duels

and fisticuffs.

*Husbands and wives fought over who
would take the family bug for a walk.*

The fashion industry offered expensive bug bonnets . . .

for both sexes.

Bug-dunking became a most popular pastime.

*The infamous Salem Bug Hunt resulted
in senseless public executions.*

The bourgeoisie favored dissections at the dinner table.

Innocent pupae were the quarry of hunters.

A few sensitive souls took it upon themselves to protect the infants from hostile crowds but were quickly branded "bugger-lovers."

Unbeknownst to their masters, the bugs
were plotting a revolt. . . .

Each day they grew more organized.

One of their leaders was arrested for treason.

His place was quickly taken by others.

Bugs began popping up everywhere—

in the most unexpected places!

Their arrogance was unsettling indeed.

Finally, the day of reckoning arrived. . . .

From a tower window the signal rang out:

A surprise attack!

The startled humans were unprepared for war.

Bug terrorists struck in the middle of the night.

A banker's child was kidnapped.

There was panic among the populace.
The situation was getting out of hand.

Rebel nests were raided and burned.

Fiendish new weapons were brought to the front.

The war took a grim turn against the insurgents.

Defections followed.

Throughout the conflict, the clergy remained neutral.

But Man's overconfidence soon took its toll. . . .

There was a shattering defeat at sea!

*At the Battle of the Bug, the human army was smashed
in a bitter confrontation. Casualties on both sides were
heavy, yet Bug hovered victorious and proud. The war
to end all wars was over.*

There was a great celebration among the victorious rebels!

At first, integration was somewhat strained.

Though their freedom had been won on the battlefield, some bugs opted for a subtle form of slavery.

Others discovered the delights of luxurious living.

In 1895, a bug went to Washington, D.C.,
determined to work within the system.

Outside a local house of ill repute, politicians were in search of a candidate for the Presidency; the deadline for nomination was drawing near, and the Party was badly disorganized.

*Suddenly, as if ordained by fate, a bug appeared in their midst.
What luck—their problem was solved! Here was a
candidate the people of the land knew nothing of. It
could surely beat the corrupt incumbent. The Party
would not perish after all!*

*The street buzzed with excitement as the new candidate
was given a quick course in handshaking.*

Speeches followed that, though lost in the translation,
were rousing.

Large crowds attended every rally.
The campaign gained momentum.

On Election Eve, success seemed certain.

The future of the world looked very bright indeed.

Finis